A Selected History of Her Heart

MARY BURRITT CHRISTIANSEN POETRY SERIES

Hilda Raz, Series Editor

The Mary Burritt Christiansen Poetry Series publishes two to four books a year that engage and give voice to the realities of living, working, and experiencing the West and the Border as places and as metaphors. The purpose of the series is to expand access to, and the audience for, quality poetry, both single volumes and anthologies, that can be used for general reading as well as in classrooms.

Also available in the Mary Burritt Christiansen Poetry Series:

The Sky Is Shooting Blue Arrows: Poems by Glenna Luschei

The Goldilocks Zone by Kate Gale

Flirt by Noah Blaustein

Progress on the Subject of Immensity by Leslie Ullman

Losing the Ring in the River by Marge Saiser

Say That by Felecia Caton Garcia

City of Slow Dissolve by John Chávez

Breaths by Eleuterio Santiago-Díaz

Ruins by Margaret Randall

Begging for Vultures: New and Selected Poems, 1994–2009 by Lawrence Welsh

Mary Burritt
Christiansen
Poetry Series

For additional titles in the Mary Burritt Christiansen Poetry Series, please visit unmpress.com.

A Selected History of Her Heart

poems

Carole Simmons Oles

University of New Mexico Press ❧ Albuquerque

Printed in the United States of America

19 18 17 16 15 14   1 2 3 4 5 6

Library of Congress Cataloging-in-Publication Data

Oles, Carole.

   [Poems. Selections]

 A selected history of her heart : poems / Carole Simmons Oles.

    pages cm. — (Mary Burritt Christiansen poetry series)

 Includes bibliographical references.

 ISBN 978-0-8263-5513-3 (pbk. : alk. paper) — ISBN 978-0-8263-5514-0 (electronic)

 I. Title.

 PS3565.L43A6 2014

 811'.54—dc23

                      2014001744

Set in Dante MT Std 11.5 / 13.5

Display type is Dante MT Std

Cover photo "Winter Fruit" and author photo courtesy of J. Murphy

In memory of Helen Kampmeyer Simmons (1911–1998) and for Logan and Beatrice.

Dig, dig; and if I come to ledges, blast.
—EDNA ST. VINCENT MILLAY

Contents

III

IV

I

Green Dance

Last night I traveled on a train, met a man
danced onstage with a troupe,

surprised at my flexibility and verve
doing the dance of broccoli.
Where the others held fans, I held
a green stalk in each hand, florets
facing out toward the audience below
like a cheerleader's pom-poms,

at the music's crescendo tore off a leaf
and sent it fluttering down
where a man could catch it—
a kind of female vegetal striptease,
a kind of male bridal bouquet—

then the tide turned as I descended
a crowd surrounded me
but not for praise as the other dancers
performed their more sinuous moves

and I woke alone and in love
with my green choreographer.

Echo Cardiogram II, at 68

Debbie says the technicians call
this machine the lemon.
It proves her point by freezing
halfway through the expedition
though I'm the one who's cold.

Shut down, it takes
five minutes of our conversation—
Planet Earth on Discovery, Alaska,
melting glaciers, frozen shoulders—
before it's ready again to land on my heart,
walk around planting flags.

This time we get to sound effects:
iambs, waves hurled at a rocky shore,
the drain backing up, sending murky
water into the daylit porcelain vessel
. . . *gobs of lost loves, the drek of ambition, self-*
loathing, fear of not/being found . . .

So soon the heart has told all
it knows. Has it ever been to school?
Or does it lurch with homeschooled
convictions, a poor Janey two-note
that nonetheless strides into March singing
not yet not yet not yet not yet not yet

Echo Cardiogram III, at 70

This time it's Pam conducting
and the machine is all warmed up.
Lights out, so the screen casts its eerie glow
vital radiance I don't crane to see.
Whatever it's doing, I don't want to jinx it—
like the boy on the magic carpet.
This life is a carpet that's faded and worn,
still I admire the design, the heft,
the color and shape it puts under my feet.
Oh. Feet.
       Can you believe they're why I'm here
again listening to the slurps and slushes
beat time? (Odd expression: as if they could beat it!)
Who ever heard of a valve infection
producing emboli on the toes?
The blood will tell, plus this test.
Mum's her word as Pam's slick transducer
circles my chest like the planchette on a ouija board,
reading messages I can't
from the wash / push of my spirited heart.

Dream after a Conversation in Venice

In which she tells me of an older friend about to divorce,
her previous lovers, his, and that he refuses
to give up the woman he claims not to love.
Then asks a few questions, which I answer throwing
crumbs the size of those on the caffé table beside us
where sparrows are pecking. Surprise on her part
that I have been alone this long.

Therefore last night I am in bed beside Enrico
at least three decades too young for me
meaning I should be about the age I was when
my own marriage was for the birds.
I stroke his arm, his cheek, but he
continues reading the newspaper.
In profile, he has the sensitive face
of Juan Diego Flórez, whom I first met
at La Scala in *La Sonnambula*.

Next I am following after Enrico
and he turns a different face to me,
suggesting we have a cigarette
(not *after*, but *instead of* sex?).
He is taller than he seemed in bed, almost too tall
and I stopped smoking for good at 40.
I think to myself perhaps we can
work out a compromise: his 3 cigarettes daily,
smoked outside the house.
Still following, I ask Do you like opera?
He throws a sharp No over his shoulder.

We sit on a bench while he takes a drag
and asks What is *degeneratively*?
A pause . . . his guess, deconstructing, Yes!
I can help with his English, he with my Italian.
Then we are out for dinner, running into
two men from my previous life. I'd introduce

Enrico, but I've forgotten his name.
The first man is now much taller
—or am I much smaller, perhaps from
a degenerative disease? I kiss his lips
leaving a lipstick smear that won't rub off
rather peels, like plastic or sunburned skin.
I hug the second man without kissing.

Enrico moves on, searching
for a table for two in a quiet corner.
But tables keep eluding us and we diverge
into a room filled only with booths.
There I greet some casual friends,
all women, one of whom joins Enrico and me.
In another still more remote space
lies a pizzeria with tables and waiters.
We choose an adjacent room
with a self-service counter.
Enrico leaves us to order
but that is the last I see of him.
And the pizza never arrives.

A Fine Example

The late cinquecento Venetian bride
displayed upon a ledge beside their bed

this marriage goblet: emerald glass, enamel
red and blue, the rim gold granules;

gilt the fluted base, the portrait bride's
curls and bodice trim, whose arc two strands

of pearls repeat—gems La Serenissima
forbade loose women. The bride's bouquet

a certain lily, her medallion frame laurel
and a Cupid pair. In women, Dolce railed,

Look not for eloquence, intelligence, talent
for living, or anything but chastity. Quaint.

More true, the bridegroom opposite his love
proclaims along a scroll *Amor vol*

fe, as any lovers might—Love
requires faith. Like light that courses
through this green Venetian glass.

Upon the Approach of My 70th Birthday, Thinking of Reincarnation

Let me come back as a Meyer lemon tree
like the one in my backyard
beside the compost bin,
lighting its lantern globes
in the darkest season,
clusters on branches that bow
like dancers warming up.

Their light overwhelms even
the security light that comes on
dawn till dusk to discourage
the man who slipped down the driveway
and robbed at gunpoint
my 90-year-old neighbor
as she sat on her bed.

Let me return each year to sharpen
the sweetness of love, also the salt
of grief and gall of betrayal.
Let me serve to celebrate life—
in mousse, marmalade, curd, Moroccan chicken
—against the latest thieving war
fighters strafing, drones off-target.

Let me join the plant kingdom next time.
Let another pick my fruit, take its essence
into her head, its oils onto his touch.

II

Blood Ritual, Age Ten

Arlene lit the match and she
held the needle in the flame
until it flickered out.
They laughed, fixing the spell
when each in turn
produced a jewel at her fingertip
and they squeezed them into one.
Amen. Now some part Jew
she wasn't just *her* self.

Crazy Love

If rain came she never felt it,
lying under umbrella trees with the boy
she was programmed to think she'd marry.
They wrapped the future in a green bandanna
and ran. Nights they'd commandeer
the playground swings and travel backward,

or watch departures from LaGuardia.
Jumbo jets roared between them, who cared
when his mother told for the girl's "own good"
how he never helped, never finished anything,
never showered—to scare the shiksa who anyway
soon left for school across the country.

Meanwhile, to grow he affected Castro,
smoked cigars and wore fatigues.
Driving to Anchorage, he wrecked the Ford
on delivery but survived to hitch home.
Once appeared beside her desk with twelve
long-stemmed curses. Once followed her
to a foreign port for proof.

Now he's the man she's alone with
in the elevator going down.
He's the face at the dining room window
that's starving. In crowds, on park paths
he waits, knowing her,
ready to kill her, ready to
shake her hand and ask what's new.

Why Morocco

1961–1962

Sweet sixteen, entering commuter college
her worst fear had been she'd never
leave her parents' three-room apartment
with the el a block away,
trains screeching in and out of her sleep.
Never sit on a sandy beach by the sea
instead of the roof, tar soaking up heat,
flocks of TV antennas overhead.
She had to defang that never.

The international schools agency offered
a U.S. Army base in Beirut
or the American School in Tangier,
English as a Foreign Language—
before ESL courses, books, labs, tapes.
She chose pulse, the heart of the city.

The marble staircase with wrought-iron railing
curved to her second-floor classroom:
high ceilings, balcony, Mediterranean breeze.
Ten students ages 12 to 16 stood
as one to greet her in various accents
and she spoke their names

Abdelatif   Consuelo   Elizabeth
Farid   Fernando   Gerardo   Josefina
Indra   Mary-Gloria   Samuel

Let us begin.

Simultaneity

Just as she was arriving on Royal Air Maroc
going through Customs, declaring herself
Institutrice, finding the cheap hotel one flight up
across from Madame Porte's tearoom
taking the room with shared bath
and Madame Concièrge a floor below,
stepping into the light toward the sea and medina
to learn where she was, what she'd done

then heading back being followed
by the Moroccan who wouldn't desist
trailed her upstairs toward her room, only leaving when
she threatened to get Madame on her first afternoon
in Tangier before sunset call to prayer

just as she was arriving, Allen Ginsberg and friends
faced into sunlight, smiled for the camera:
Orlovsky, Burroughs, Ansen, Sommerville, Bowles
already writing their '60s adventures
but they were the guys, they had each other
valid artistic licenses, mutual experiments—
Ginsberg captioned the photo . . . *mysterious-haired* . . .
earnest . . . resolute . . . Villa Muneria garden, Tanger July 1961

she knew nothing of them, they had nothing to do with
her stretched on the cot in the windowless room
from which tomorrow she would set out, rent
her furnished third-floor apartment at 10 rue Savigny
overlooking the beach, the hawkers. Her *Villa Experiencia*.

Mimosa

Latin paints its essence: *mimus* mime
and *pudicus* bashful, modest, chaste.

On the Old Mountain, spilling down to the sea
Mimosa pudica, fragrant as dreams of escape.

Eyes closed, she buried her face in the globes
of yellow. Tender leaves shrank from her praise.

How to sense when they're touched as blessing,
when to shrink guarding fragrance and gold?

Pursued

She'd just returned from the souk
when crazy love boy appeared from New York

miniaturized in the eye of her door.
Behind it she stood holding her breath.

She waited all day for him to quit
the hill where he sat staring

at her apartment, finally leaving
just before dark to catch the ferry out.

Son of an Immigrant Butcher in Queens

where they both grew up, he visited,
rented a Simca, took her to Tetouan,
bargained for babouches for her sister
and taught her to drive a manual shift.

Thanks to him she could rent the blue VW
journey south with her colleague Ruth
40 years older, already retired
from a Jersey City school.

Thanks to him for having played Mozart,
led her to his MIT prof
at a class on *The Marriage of Figaro*.
Would there be marriage for them?

He was a man who fed others,
a man who mapped cities, people.
A mind like a laser—before lasers.
The temperature of a group of particles

is indicative of the level of excitation.
He was never cold, even
in harsh New England winters
wore only a sports coat.

So why not?
She wanted to hide, he wanted to seek.
Once they had lain beside each other.
They would stay childhood sweethearts.

Falling Bodies

I

Of these sweethearts' bodies
whose the more tortured—
his, spine wrenched at birth
or hers, cinctured
by Catholic shame?
He superseded his by will, trust
a mind bodying forth with delight.
How could she redeem hers?
Not through denial: her mother
and doctor made her eat.
No way to body's perfection.
She had yet to discover
her route, where it led.

2

Just her age, Maryse
arrived in Tangier from Dakar
her former lycée post.
Teachers far from Dijon
and New York, they shared
stories, films in two languages,
the Englishman's Indian food
and their tears streaming down.
Petite, trim . . . yet
Maryse lamented her *cellulite*.
To purge the deposit
suffered weekly bondage
encased in a plastic suit.

Object Lesson: Trying to Translate

Curious American like the victim,
she took notes on small onionskin
sheets marked *Paris-Dakar*
an Eiffel Tower forming the *i*,
both words embracing a globe.
March 24, 1962—more than two years
after the crime, the girl's belongings
lined up at the front of the cold room.

The trial for rape and murder
was conducted in French,
language of government and business still.
Radiateurs inutiles, she wrote, practicing.
Personal representative of the Minister
of Islamic Affairs, the reporter
from *Al-Istiqlal* leaned forward.
Where were the American papers?

The prosecutor circled, an eagle
with white ruff around his polished head,
well-tended, long white talons ready to tear.
The judge's cheeks had collapsed
but his mouth wouldn't be moved.
Closing in, the lawyer cited
the length of cord found at the scene.
The psychiatrist gave his expert opinion.

The accused, English but named Moore
had eyes afloat on dark half-moons.
Did a guard make that red spot on his cheek,
a spider bite while he slept?
Could he sleep?
As ordered, Moore rose to confront the witness.
Their eyes met. *Oui. C'est lui.*
Now the judge smiled.

"No one wants to see this,"
she started to write
but stopped. Wasn't it just
what they'd all come to see—
foreigners, women, journalists seated,
Moroccan men against the walls,
she herself, taking notes—
this burlap sack held high?

The witness swore he'd sold Moore the sack
several days before Fête du Trône.
But Moore claimed he bought it the 19th!
Air began to leak out of him . . .
his brow furrowed, his mouth cinched
as if pulled by a cord
when the prosecutor showed
the girl's green plaid skirt.

Marrakech, the Souk

Every bend lured them deeper
into the labyrinth—
smells of donkeys, cedar, sizzling lamb
brilliant patterns of rugs, glint of copper and brass
sliding intervals from an oud
in alleys narrowing, emptying into each other,
doubling back . . .

Enchanted out of their sense of direction
the two blonde women in headscarves,
perhaps mother and daughter, tried
not to look lost, tried to become
invisible even as they drank in
all the souk displayed and concealed.
They had to turn toward the voice

behind them, the handsome, clean-shaven,
short-haired Moroccan in Western dress
greeting them in German. They corrected
American. He deployed a few English words,
then retreated to flawless French.
The young woman's eyes filled with his smile,
the old one squinted, assessing this

Mohammed, nephew of a local sharif
invoked as character witness.
Army lieutenant visiting, may he invite them
to his cousin's shop for mint tea?
May he escort them through the intricate maze?
No less charmed than the snakes in Djema el Fna
they accepted, milked of defense.

And later, may he take the young one out dancing?

The Ditch

Early next morning, after the dancing,
the struggle in his car, her resistance
that tried to stay friends

she joined the other women
driving north. Exhausted, she took her turn
at the wheel of their VW bus.
Later, when Miss Byers asked *Stop*, she veered,
hit the shoulder too fast, skidded
right wheels into the ditch.

No one hurt, no damage to the bus.
But they were stuck.
In the middle of a Moroccan nowhere,
stuck.
Her cheeks burned: her first driving mishap.
Before cell phones, no triple A, what could they do?

Wait for three men on donkeys to drift over,
curious, sizing things up, devising a plan.
Hitching two donkeys to the front bumper,
one man conducted, two pushed from the back
as they hauled. The emptied bus lurched
forward, up, onto firm ground.

Firmer than where she stood, shamed.
The ditch, the struggle—
like stars aligning in her chart.

On Leave

When Mohammed the lieutenant had leave
he drove his Renault to Tangier.
From her balcony they watched a freighter dock,
she photographed his flashy smile.

They drank mint tea on the mountain
sharing the view of the bay
with the café owner's monkey.
They must have talked, or tried to.

That night in her kitchen
he cooked them sheep brains in tomatoes—
disgusted, she ate.
In her mother's kitchen she refused to eat liver.

Later at the hotel on the beach they danced
to Ray Charles' "Am I Blue."
The air smelled of orange blossoms and ozone.
Soon it would rain.

Blood Bond

Mohammed told the German doctor
Ich habe angst.
For her, bleeding, or for himself?
But the doctor wouldn't report this.

She didn't know how to do it
and he didn't know how not to.
And conversely.
She was one in a million.

At the Croissant-Rouge
a Sister of Mercy held her hand
un deux trois quatre till she sank.
She woke with him on a cot beside her
eating the *biscottes* Sister had left.

His pidgin English, her pidgin French . . .
her body spanned nations,
the world's great religions—
now they'd understand.
Now peace would reign.

To Visit Him

She walked in darkness
to the bus station—a woman walking alone
in a place in the world where she shouldn't.
The streets almost empty
she was alone on the bus
till it began stopping at villages—
a man climbed on with a basket of baguettes
a woman with a sack full of clementines.
Arriving, was this the right station? No him.
In broken French, she phoned the caserne.
They regretted—*Il est mis en congé.*
Yes, she knew. That's why they'd agreed to meet.
Or she thought that was what they'd said,
language hobbling between them.
A Moroccan man overheard,
invited her home to his wife and children.
Her faith was rewarded:
parents, children, the stranger met
in a tajine of language, gestures, expressions
over couscous and syrupy tea.
They insisted she stay on their couch
where she slept grateful, undisturbed,
in the open hand of Islam.

Revelation in Ifrane

At a remote ski lodge in the Atlas Mountains
with his friends, against his religion
Mohammed drank alcohol, curled his lip
fought with them in Arabic.
What good were her sensible shoes
and handbag containing a U.S. passport.
Her schoolmarm's chignon and small French.
What did he believe after all?
What did she?

Revelation in Meknes

Enfin, this truth he would tell, the photo:
a baby balanced on the French mama's knee.

She could have been looking at herself.

At least this wasn't her parents' life.

Her Phone Rang

Mohammed called long-distance *cent*
soixante treize soixante et un
and she answered for the last time. The phone
on the wall gave a view to the Mediterranean
which she'd cross to sail home from Lisbon.
She breathed deeply   *Je ne peux point*
continuer. He asked if she'd met someone
else. *Non,* she lied.   The least of her sins.

Closing Argument, Considering Blood

Was it rape, date rape to use the current term—or did she ask for it—to use the crude vernacular.

Look at him: a handsome young Moslem, lieutenant in the Moroccan Army, intelligent, probably from a good family (he told her his uncle was a sharif in Marrakech), handsome as we already said, with a healthy libido and a view of Western women gained from Hollywood, popular songs, and their short skirts, uncovered hair, degrees, travels alone.

Look at her: raised a Catholic, leaving the fold at 16 but brought up on virginal myths unprepared for real life as she found it—that, and wanting to please, always always deferring to the wishes of others, like her mother before her . . . head down on the kitchen table when the man who drank too much made them cry.

Still, she must have halfway known what might happen in her third-floor flat at 10 rue Savigny on the narrow bed. Yet how could she know all that blood wasn't the sign of a second passage into womanhood, the towels sopping it up weren't the normal price for pleasure or what someone deemed pleasure—not what she'd felt:

the collision of bodies, cultures, opportunity and motive, innocence and experience, resistance and compliance, irresistible force and moveable object? Give him this: he stayed, took her to the hospital, didn't let her bleed to death. *Ich habe angst*, he told the German doctor, and we can see why.

Was it her fault? Was it his? Was it in their blood? Or shall we close the case. Set them both free.

Replay, Her Phone Rang

Mohammed's call long-distance to *cent*
soixante treize soixante et un
rang in her head, on the phone
with a view to the Mediterranean
she'd cross to sail west from Lisbon.
She breathed deeply.   *Je ne peux point . . .*
she repeated. Another man? She lied again.
Libre.   To save her own skin.

Her Lie: The Polish Chess Player

Nazis advancing, the Polish chess player's parents
had fled with their infant son
to Tangier—international zone, free port
historical gateway of every traffic.
When France fell, her colonies clicked
into line with the Axis, shook the Jews' haven
until the Allies invaded, 1942.

When she met him two decades later
his mother wore fur, his father's practice thrived.
Soon he would leave them to make his own fortune
in her country, city by the Charles.
Some chess moves later, some wine, some films
some foreplay later she would discern
she had no place in this plan.
Was she blue? She could have predicted—
for his winning game, he'd need
the perfect queen.

Historical Interlude: Eavesdropping on Hell

Axis covert intelligence agents, located in Spanish-controlled Tangier,
reported that the Jews, along with communists, and Allied internees
in the newly liberated regions of French North Africa, had been freed
from the numerous concentration and labor camps established by Vichy.
Jews held in French detention camps in North Africa numbered
about 15,000 out of a population of 295,000.

The Axis agents also reported that the prohibitions against Jews
in governmental service and the schools had been lifted
though removal of these sanctions only occurred months after
the Allies had liberated French North Africa. The new regime
under Admiral Jean Darlan and General Henri Giraud declined
to abrogate the Statutes des Juifs immediately after liberation,
claiming that to remove the laws would incite the Arab population.

However, Moslems as a group steadfastly and consistently had refused
to participate in Vichy's anti-Jewish program.
In fact many of the Moslem elite openly had supported the Jews.*

---

* Robert J. Hanyok, *Eavesdropping on Hell: Historical Guide to Western Communications Intelligence and the Holocaust, 1939–1945*, 2nd ed. (Fort Meade, MD: Center for Cryptologic History, National Security Agency, 2005).

Praise Song for Her Student Samuel

If the gods had eyelashes
they'd be the eyelashes of Samuel
lush black fringe made to vanquish

If they had eyes
they'd be polished ebony heartwood
deep as the eyes of Samuel

Over that dazzle of darkness
those touchy protectors
two raven arcs

would poise on white satin—
shields from sun and rain
flags of internal weather

Praise the boy Samuel
his laugh, his arm around Abdelatif
Samuel of the lineage of Abitbol

Moroccan family of rabbis, dayanim
Talmudists—leaders
of the Jewish community of Sefrou

Praise *abitbol* a drum
calling down the ages
beating in the singer's breast

With Her the Earrings

The verb "have" does not exist in Arabic.

A Frenchman owned the antiquities shop
on Boulevard Mohammed V—treasures
looted in the old days of colonialism
or bartered cheap in a smoky bazaar.
Four gold square coins transgressed into earrings
Arabic covering the surface, invocations
neither she nor the Frenchman
could read. She wasn't thinking
of their dubious provenance, or what her
purchase would add to insult or theft.
They were exotic mementos to possess,
medals for service
in a difficult campaign.
Monnaie Marocaine Frappée a Sabta
au 12–13th siècle before
Spain took the port in 1580.
The coins, stolen more than once,
so too the town where they were struck—
Roman colony, then Arab, Portuguese, Spanish.
The Moroccans want it back.
Men fadlak, take the earrings too.
With her what she remembers,
these coins of her realm.

Ruth Who Fed Her Dates

stuffed with La vache qui rit
as she drove on dirt roads to Erfoud
Who stood between her and the mayor
a mother lion when he curled his tongue out
in a lewd invitation

Who walked up and down hills
over stones, in alleys and souks
everywhere in those British Brevits
eager but tough, rationing smiles
Who carried a small silver flask to Fes

Ruth who rolled her eyes at how
stupid she was, who forgave her
Who waited until she was sure
the girl would leave at the end of the year
before informing her that she would stay

Who next taught in Istanbul
had varicose vein surgery in New Jersey
lived in London a decade
while the girl sent back word from a Boston suburb
Who lived last in Red Bank, New Jersey

always reaching—this concert, that play
or museum in Manhattan, *Times* articles on Morocco
Ruth, longest surviving graduate
of the first Human Ecology majors at Cornell
Ruth who died at 103

40 years after they first met teaching
on rue de Belgique, kindred travelers
Ruth who should have seen the new president
and his Christian, Moslem, Jewish,
Kenyan, Indonesian, African American, white family

Ruth, Unitarian Universalist who practiced Rumi

Find me near the flower's eye
that takes in provocation
and begins to grow.

III

Photo of a Girl Fourteen: Merrill, Wisconsin, 1925

Spring wind blows her scarf
but her gaze is unruffled,
a moody look renowned
as adolescence. She poses
against a telephone pole,
weight on her left leg
her right bent at the knee.
Hands in overalls pockets,
wool sweater underneath,
scarf the attention of a girl
who knows how to dress.
The overalls are much too long—
maybe one of her brother's?—
but she makes the 4-inch cuff
seem the new rage from Paree.
Her flair shows from head to toe:
the cloche hat with pleats,
the two-toned leather, pointy shoes.
She's a farm girl who wants
to split for the city.
Who could blame her?
—the bare, muddy yards, gray
clumps in the narrow road.
And not a leaf yet on those two trees
outside the plain white house;
those sheds out back with planks
leaning drunk against the walls.
She's the only one here
except the photographer, she's
the most interesting sight for miles.
Her brunette hair matches
the dark seeds of her eyes.
One side of it behaves, the other tries
to escape in a curl like a question.
Ah and her left strap has fallen,
as if she's already begun to shed

overalls for something more chic.
How can she know what flight holds?
the 3-room apartment a block from the el,
kitchen full of scrubbed long johns dangling
from the ceiling like a row of hanged men,
dumbwaiter raised up from the basement,
the husband's shot glass,
the ration stamps, miscarriages, lost boy—
what flight holds in that lifetime
fourteen full years later, wherein
she'll bear down, expel me.

From Afar, Constructing My Birth Day

January 7

The woman lists to the porcelain sink, rides
the crest of her pain. True alarm!
her husband runs downstairs for a cab
(they don't yet have a phone), she snaps
shut the lock on her suitcase, in the taxi
gasps—not at snow on the windshield.
The man feels all lights arrest them. This
is their first, a beginner gave them the slip.
When the cab arrives, he is red-faced,
thick-fingered: his wallet's at home.
She has to pay. They climb steps
the godmother soon will fall down, laughing
at the infant's red topknot geyser.
I am that note in their bottle, washed here.

The Compact

We're all reading yearbooks in the attic
and e-mailing madly to concoct
our fiftieth anniversary high school reunion

so I'm back in 1955, opening
the wrap on a mother-of-pearl
compact, cunning squares of iridescence
fit together over gleaming gold.

Do I even wear face powder?
I think only our mothers do.
We wear the shine
of our over-industrious glands.

No matter. It's a gift, unexpected, from the one

who makes my stomach flip,
my cheeks burn red as flares.
A mirror inside, but I don't want to look:
face reveals what I need to hide.

Half a century later, things things so many lost
things, the compact among them.
Let it return to the sea.

For him: these found breaths on a mirror.

The Beginning

Her ex has all the slides
but in her head she has an afternoon
on a hillside in Mykonos,
drinking Demestica from the bottle
while the Mediterranean flashes
as if to ignite the prickly grass
or send signals she's not decoding.
They've eaten every morsel,
goat cheese and torn bread,
and no one expects them
anywhere.

But the thorn in his finger
is becoming infected; by the time
they reach Rome a *dottore*
will have to be summoned.
Still, tonight after lamb in their favorite *tabepna*
they lie together
in the narrow bed near waves.
Tomorrow, *Efcharisto*, when she steps
into the olive-green Hush Puppies loafers
under her side of the bed
she is pregnant with their son.

Definition: Northern California Autumn

To my grandson Logan

The flowers whose blooming I missed
in my garden when I walked Vermont beside
you tapping the walls of your mother
then knocking hard
before we all breathed the one
sunset over Lake Champlain
those flowers are blooming again, more profuse
for the cool nights, still more
sweet for the hummingbirds whose choice
Mexican salvia raises high
purple torches to light
the shortening days

as your face slips further
beyond the stratosphere I traveled
home—where my house is—
to this place I call exile, far
from you who wear my maiden name.
Last night when I reached
you shrank, began to melt . . .
waking, in a green book I ranged
your photos, page after page enlarged you
restored your mouth whistling, sucking, singing hosannas
to your mama my child, now
someone new

tied to me by more than blood
commothers, matrifilipeers
let the language expand to record
our newborn relation

and joy to its maker, you
you buster, you redheaded you

Ode for the City

          Manhattan not mine
across the East River where, from the fence
at Astoria Park, I gazed as rats scrambled below.
Magical city over the Queensboro Bridge
with its slippery-when-wet grating buried
in macadam, boyfriends' cars traveled
too fast to win you, slid us toward the rails.
Approaching high above the natural moat
we could peer into rich windows on Beekman Place.
City across the river tunneled into from heights
of Queensboro Plaza, the BMT's earsplitting
curve above traffic, the laws of physics
might send the train flying like Mercury
over tarred rooftops to land in the Village.

Oh train that took me out of the attached
rubber-stamped houses inside which nothing
could happen, train with orange plastic seats
and the marks of my fellow riders: gum,
paper, news, phlegm, and assorted invisible longings.
That took me to Central Park with my friends
and my ice skates where we stayed till
our cheeks burned with cold and the dizziness
of holding hands, one moving body
as we took the rink. Then converged on
Schrafft's or Joey's, any coffee shop on Fifth,
ordered hot chocolate and sat in a booth
laughing too loud till grown-ups stared,
threw down their napkins and left.

How I tried to be grown-up, falling for
Gordon MacRae, tenor with an Amherst degree.
Wearing the purple suit mother made, pinning
a gardenia to the lapel and boarding the BMT
for the Palace, his concert the fan club
was sworn to attend. After the show we stood

in line backstage for Gordie's name
scrawled on a program or in our diaries.
He was signing while swigging
a beer—like my father. The End.
Ah generation of ignorance and unconsciousness.
Duck-and-cover generation, who never inquired
the price of our magical city of maybes, our cauldron
of desire, disappointment, and constant surprise.

I thought I'd never leave Purgatory Queens
but surprise!—came Berkeley, Morocco,
Cambridge. Never reaching The
City for good. After its darkest day
Silence for the dead
at Easter, Trinity Church rang with lilies like inverted bells,
resurrection on everyone's mind.
In my private skyline, on this ground I build
the tallest tower, a new UN headquarters.
Tower of books, seeds, cures;
tower of debating, yielding and shaking hands.
Of breaking pita, rye, brioche, nan.
Later ice-skating in kaftans, saris, dashikis, Brooks Brothers—
        round and round, getting the rhythm of the glide.

IV

Notes to Beatrice: The Beginning

viator, viatrix L., wayfarer

I

Strong heartbeat, head down, nearly ready
reports your father from across an ocean
about you there in your own salt sea

you into whose ear he chants paeans
and unlikely American folk songs
mixing their music with your mother's mother tongue.

Viaggiatrice, traveler, in my California garden this morning
the first purple iris unfurled her message from the gods.

II

You float as the plane splits the clouds
en route toward your parents' Swedish friends,
the last flight you and your mother are allowed.

Her seat belt vanishes under the belly where you extend
an elbow, a foot, testing your muscles and her walls.
Hello out there, thousands

of miles from your father's mother. Hello, aestival
girl—come to our arms, your new home.
Buying my ticket to Amsterdam, I guess at your schedule—

two doctors disagreed. You'll take your good time.
Your mother does yoga, walks daily, cooks healthy ragù.

III

Today I went to Harvard Square to bag
a utilitarian and beautiful shirt
for your mother to wear nursing

you. Not so easy to find a 100 percent
real natural fabric, instead of some "modal"
unknown, undefined that I wouldn't want—

no matter what latest color or style—
touching your precious, natural skin.

IV

On Mass. Ave., cross-legged on the bricks, a man
with long hair and beard, head bowed on his chest
the basket before him holding some coins

beside him a dog and a sign that arrests:
Homeless Vegetarian. I have to laugh
to myself though I find no humor in homelessness

or hunger either. But why shouldn't he ask
benefactors to respect his dietary and moral
convictions? Around a corner, Psalm 46

carved in stone prevails:
God is in the midst of the city.

V

Last February in Rome, in Piazza del Popolo
in your mother, around you a million Italians
crying, *Se non ora, quando?*

meaning now is the time to spurn
Il Cavaliere, the *repubblica*'s national shame,
leering offense to its women

and honorable citizens. Hear them claim
power to the people. *Senti: Il Popolo c'e tu.*

VI

I'm hearing Ralph Vaughan Williams' cantata at MIT—
where your parents met—praying for peace
through the drum-rolls of war, today

as in 1935. You there in your peaceful
orb, soon-to-be Beatrice: *Dona nobis pacem*
for your sake. Let all

nations be gathered together, balm
for the soiled world   a single human voice.

VII

Meanwhile, attending live opera in utero, your joy
is palpable. You waltz to *Der Rosenkavalier*
inside your snug ballroom, trying

its limits, you hear the name that might be yours—
Sophie a candidate—you don't understand
the idea of lost youth, just ¾ time and the Italian tenor

in your blood and the sound
of three women's singing, accepting mystery.

VIII

Uniform motion problems are nothing compared to this
time-distance puzzle: C travels from Boston
to Haarlem June 23rd (returning July 5th)

B travels toward her sometime between
June 21st and July 1st—even two doctors can't tell
so I guess too, get plane

tickets hoping we intersect, solve for all variables,
and I see you sweetening our air with your breath.

IX

Arriving at 6 a.m., riding the airport bus west
to Haarlem station where your father will meet me
I'm impressed by the order of separate paths

for cars, buses, bikes; the neat rows of houses and trees.
When I descend at the station
Dutch people are rushing to work while I lean

on my suitcase waiting in the chilly sun.
Then here he is, carrying a bag of croissants
for breakfast. We walk home through green

the park beside the canal, curve down
the hill, cross the bridge, enter your street,
stop at your door, climb one

steep Dutch flight to greet
your mother and *you*—an amazing presence
requiring adjustments of balance and spatial feats

of avoidance wondrous and immense.
Often she strokes her *pancia*, entreating
you to come the short distance

between us. Here at table the blue seat
awaits you, here you can unfurl who you are.

X

"Walks"—understatement!—five days before you burst forth we hike ten kilometers to Bloemendaal aan zee, Zandvoort, against a stiff breeze off the North Sea, under brilliant sun, with the dunes to ourselves, stopping halfway at a visitors' center filled with exhibits and schoolchildren, much farther on emerging from the dunes we veer uphill toward the beach, passing an old man on a bike stopped to rest at a bus shelter and a biking family of four, the youngest has taken a spill, weeps, brushes off her bloody knee and remounts as we push uphill toward smells of food frying, staple aroma of beaches everywhere, then past several stands and restaurants stop at the one that offers the best view of the sea, sheltered tables outside, a long bench of cushions with their backs to the sea and plexiglass panels that defend from the bracing, uproarious air we drink beer and eat Dutch snacks, take more photos—in which your mother (and you) languishes against cushions like a pasha—we descend to the beach where while your parents (and you) walk ahead I bend for shells and find sundry treasure such as this petrified wood studded with tiny barnacles and bristly grass hairs that looks at me now from my desk restoring that day, our hike, you soon to appear amid us under those massive, tumbling white clouds exactly what Dutch painters capture.

XI

"Soon to appear"—but when? I leave tomorrow!
I trusted your own good time and must still.
We have pizza in the bistro garden with your *nonna*

and *nonno* just here from Rome. As we part beside the steeple
of St. Bavo's, your mother asks me should they call
if she goes into labor tonight. Of course! Anything's possible.

Baci all around and I return to my hotel
aerie where packed bags stand ready. My uneven sleep
is marked by St. Bavo's chiming the hours faithfully.

I'm up at 6 and ready to go when the phone chirps:
My son from the hospital—where you three have worked
since 4:30—announcing today you will complete your trip . . .

Arrive just as I depart? No way! I'll tack,
change course, change ticket—meet you, Beatrice.
My bags and I ride to the airport and back.

Now, patience. I'll soon see your face,
dearest traveler taking the journey of your life.

⌒

How to pass hours when all I can think of is your safe
arrival? Too early for the Historical Museum
but I set out, stop to watch workmen loaf

beside the canal while you too navigate a canal home.
You're with me at the archival photo exhibit
—schoolgirls led across a field by a nun,

Ku Klux Klan members riding, a shot
from above into a town square where Nazis fire
at Dutch citizens taking cover behind a lamppost

while a two-year-old follows her
shadow over the cobblestones.

෨

Sandwich and a beer at Grand Café Brinkman.
My phone hasn't rung yet so back to the hotel
room to wait. Finally, late afternoon, my son

to say he's looking at my granddaughter, her full
head of dark, curly hair. Born just an hour before
and everyone fine, tired, hale.

Now I dash to the station again, catch the bus for
VU Medical Center in Amsterdam. Find Delivery 8C.

෨

All eyes on you. We all lean in to see
you at your mother's breast, both learning how
to nurse. Your parents and three

grandparents are the *we*, so you know
you're not *sola*. We belong to each other.
I can feel a letting down in my own

breast—was it really all those years
ago? Darling girl, I find your makers reflected
in your brand-new face never before

seen on this earth. Beatrice, love, can we be connected
across continents and tongues?

෨

We give you and your parents time alone
these hours before you're released to start
your first night in the world at home.
I'm back in Haarlem for the concert
on St. Bavo's famed Christian Müller 3-meter-tall organ
once played by ten-year-old Mozart,

by Handel and Mendelssohn.
Tonight its 5,068 pipes and 68 voices sing
your name, under the fingers and feet of Eric Lebrun.

Psalm 81: Liturgy for a festival. Raise a song,
sound the timbrel, the sweet lyre with the harp.
I hear a voice I had not known.

       ‽

Here in my garden the ruby-throated hummingbird darts
doing midair
needlepoint in hibiscus, salvia, orange trumpets . . .

May you, dear Beatrice, drink the wonder
of this day.

Maple in Space

red redder reddest

incomparable tree
there with stodgy evergreens

you surge
while they retreat

only you know the dance
only you the pagoda

a swatch of red in flight bisects you
in its throat it turns a rusty key

the adjectival air swings out

        to let us through

The Cedar Waxwing

What keeps the full weight of my foot
from striking the welcome mat
as I open the door
and stride into morning?
What I so nearly crush belongs
airborne, delivering song
over my third-story porch rail,
not here, not feathers from peril
where I, just in time, stop.

I try to reconstruct luck—
the failure of screen door to break
such small bones—or misfortune:
sun at an angle, bird's collision
with window or wall. Perhaps my brute
inattention caused the hurt
I just almost compounded infinitely.
Bird won't move, so I do, bending low
holding my unwieldy breath

to touch the clenched claws, stroke
once the head. Nothing. The black
glass stares. I've never been this close
to a life that ought to rise
from my huge look at its fear.
Crest, black mask, tan-feathered
body, two sparks on a yellow-
dipped tail, paler yellow
under the breast disappearing—

can I rescue such beauty?
Pride and autumn make me try.
She's breathing: webs that hang
on branches. To be spare wings,
my fingers close around her.
A hand's evolved to lift a damaged bird

and hold it till whatever.
I feel the voltage under feathers.
          I open my palm.

ACKNOWLEDGMENTS

The following poems in this volume originally appeared in these journals:

"Definition: Northern California Autumn," *Alaska Quarterly Review*
"The Compact," "Green Dance," and "Upon the Approach of My 70th
Birthday, Thinking of Reincarnation," *bosque (the magazine)*
"The Beginning," *Connecticut Review*
"Ode for the City," *Consequence*
"A Fine Example," *Painted Bride Quarterly*
"Maple in Space," *Prairie Schooner*
"Photo of a Girl Fourteen: Merrill, Wisconsin, 1925," the *Women's
Review of Books*

All poems in part II except "Crazy Love," "Falling Bodies," and
"Simultaneity" were published in *Prairie Schooner*, some in slightly
different form.

"The Cedar Waxwing" appeared in the Bread Loaf anthology *Poems for
a Small Planet: Contemporary American Nature Poetry*, edited by Robert
Pack and Jay Parini (Hanover, NH: Middlebury College Press, 1993).

Also by
Carole Simmons Oles